Great advice from two outstanding leaders in their field. This book, when read and followed, will put money in your bank.

**Don Green**
CEO, Napoleon Hill Foundation

PRESENTED TO

_____

FROM

_____

DATE

_____

# PASSPORT
## TO
# SUCCESS

DR. GREG REID'S TOP 10 NATIONAL BEST SELLERS

*Three Feet From Gold*
*Positive Impact*
*The Millionaire Mentor*
*Thoughts Are Things*
*Wealth Made Easy*
*Success and Something Greater*
*Napoleon Hill's Road to Riches*
*Stickability*
*Sellership*
*The Tokens*

PRODUCER OF THE OSCAR-QUALIFIED FILM

*Wish Man*

*Experience Next Level Living*

# JIM STOVALL
# DR. GREG REID

Published and distributed by:
SOUND WISDOM
P.O. Box 310
Shippensburg, PA 17257-0310
717-530-2122

info@soundwisdom.com

www.soundwisdom.com

ISBN 13 TP: 978-1-64095-394-9

ISBN 13 eBook: 978-1-64095-395-6

For Worldwide Distribution, Printed in the U.S.A.

1 2 3 4 5 6 7 8 / 26 25 24 23 22

# CONTENTS

# FOREWORD

We've heard it said that during challenging times in life, "When things feel like they're falling apart, they are actually falling into place." It takes great courage to step outside our comfort zone and take a chance on creating a life that is beyond our current reality, to achieve our wildest dreams.

Many people let fear stop them, and it isn't until a great life challenge presents itself that we may finally step into the fear and move through to the other side. It is only then that we can tap into our unfulfilled potential, and if we can stay the course, we'll come out victorious as our most valuable selves. We can then emerge as the version of us that can create lasting change in the lives of others.

I encourage you to not only read the words within these pages, but to live the principles. Allow yourself to chip away that which is no longer serving you so that you too may discover the masterpiece that lies within.

Get started now. With each step you take, you will grow stronger and stronger, more and more skilled, more and more self-confident, and more and more successful.

**Mark Victor Hansen**
Co-author for the *Chicken Soup for the Soul*
and the *Ask!* book series

# CHAPTER ONE

Alex's deep slumber was disturbed by a familiar rumbling, but one he couldn't place. As he fought off the fog of sleep, he slowly recognized the sound of drawers being opened and closed. His thoughts immediately turned to the suspicion that there was an intruder in his apartment.

Quietly, he propped himself up on his elbows as his eyes struggled to adapt to the dim light and tried to gauge where the sound was coming from. His fear shifted to relief as he recognized the silhouette standing in front of the dresser was his girlfriend, Katie, as she transferred clothes from the dresser to a suitcase on the edge of the bed.

"Hey, what are you doing up so early?" he asked. "And why are you packing a suitcase? Are you going on a trip?"

"I couldn't sleep," she replied in a voice devoid of emotion. "Actually, I've been up most of the night."

Sitting upright, with a sense of concern, Alex asked his girlfriend of more than two years, "What's the matter? Do you feel okay?"

"I'm fine. But we're not." Then taking a pause and a deep breath, she finished her thought, "Alex, I'm leaving you."

"What?" her boyfriend stammered, not sure if he'd heard her correctly. "What do you mean, you're leaving?"

"Oh, it looks like I finally got your attention," Katie smirked. "But it's a little too late—far too late, as a matter of fact. Let's face it Alex, this relationship isn't going anywhere. It took me long enough to figure it out, but I finally did."

Dazed and confused, Alex was at a loss for words. It was the first he'd heard that she wasn't happy, and her revelation took him by total surprise.

"I don't get it. You can't possibly think this is *my* fault! If you weren't happy, why didn't you say something—anything?"

"I shouldn't have to, Alex," she whispered gently under her breath, yet loud enough to be heard.

"You know, I can't read minds. I can't do anything about whatever is bothering you if you don't tell me. Come on," he said, patting the bed beside him, "Sit down and let's talk."

"It's too late for talking, Alex. It's useless, really. We don't want the same things. It's best that we go our separate ways."

Alex noticed that there was a sense of finality in her voice, and he began to grasp the fact that she was serious.

"What do you mean we don't want the same things? What is it that you want?" he asked.

With a tear in her eye, she choked on her words, and with real sadness in her voice, she told him exactly what she wanted.

"I wanted it all. Marriage. Children. A home in the suburbs— the storybook life."

"I feel blindsided here; why didn't you come out and say something? I had no idea. I thought everything was good the way it is," he replied, not trying to hide his growing frustration.

A slight tone of anger was evident as she sputtered, "I've been trying to tell you this whole time, but you don't even see what's right in front of your eyes. Everything is always about you. I just wanted a little to be about us."

Not knowing what to say, he glanced back at Katie and wondered how her disappointment and unhappiness could be so obvious to her and a mystery to him at the same time.

He never meant to hurt her feelings, and truth be told, she wasn't wrong—the image of two kids, a dog, and a mortgage was the furthest thing from his mind, especially since his job had ended the month before and he hadn't had any income since.

"Katie, you're just overtired. Don't make any rash decisions. We can work this out," Alex suggested. "Besides, you don't have anywhere to go."

"Are you kidding me?" she said, her exasperation loud and clear. "For thirty days straight I've been leaving the classifieds on the coffee table. I even circled the ones I called about! Really, Alex, you don't pay attention to anything I do. I might as well be living alone. And that's what I intend to do."

Grabbing her suitcases, she turned on her heel and walked out the door. After all the time they'd been together, she left without as much as a goodbye. There was no "Thanks for the memories, I'm sorry it had to end this way." Nothing. Just the sting of her last words saying she'd rather be alone than to stay with him and wish she was.

Feeling overwhelmed, Alex wondered again how it was possible that he hadn't seen this coming. What had gone wrong, and why was he the last one to know?

Different scenarios ran through his mind as he contemplated what he could have done differently. Then he remembered that he had a job interview that morning. If it were any other job, he'd call and cancel the interview. But not today—this was *the* job, the one he really wanted and had worked toward for years.

*There is no way I'm going to risk losing this opportunity,* he thought. *I can deal with Katie later. It's probably a good idea to let her cool down for a day or two, anyway.*

◆–––––––◆–––––––◆

Punctuality was never an issue for Alex, and today was no exception. He once read that leaders always show up early, as it's their vision and mission they hope others will follow. The managers of the world tend to show up on time and are in charge of opening the doors for others; on the other hand, employees of the world tend to show up late.

Arriving for the interview fifteen minutes before scheduled, Alex was proud of himself as he took the time to admire his surroundings and imagined working for one of the most innovative and revered tech companies in the area. Not only did he think he was perfect for the job, but he also believed the company was perfect for him.

They were leading pioneers in employee-employer relations and offered phenomenal benefits, including bonuses and paid time to invest in personal interests. It was a community-centered company and among the top twenty places to work, according to several prestigious national surveys.

*Working here wouldn't even feel like work,* Alex thought. *I got this! There is no way I'm going to mess this up.*

Straightening what he always referred to as his "power tie," he approached the silver circular information desk. "Good morning," he smiled at the receptionist. "My name is Alex Best. I have a 9 a.m. interview."

"Good morning, Mr. Best. Please have a seat on the sofa in the lobby, and he'll meet you there," she said, pointing across the room. "You're a few minutes early, but I believe he's about ready for you."

Noting that a man sat in a chair positioned close to one arm of the couch, Alex opted to sit on the opposite end, as far away as he could. He opened his briefcase and pulled out fresh, crisp copies of his resume to hand to his interviewer as he went over some of the points he wanted to make during the interview. Being a bit egotistical, he even attached a head shot to the front cover, showing off his trademark smile.

The man in the chair across from him cleared his throat.

"Hello, I'm Tom, and you are…?"

"Um, Alex," he replied without looking up, as he continued shuffling through his papers like a deck of playing cards.

"It's nice to meet you. Beautiful day out there, isn't it? How's your morning been?"

*Great. Just great,* Alex thought to himself. *The biggest interview of my life, and I get to sit next to Chatty Chad over here who won't leave me alone.*

For the first time, Alex raised his head and looked at the stranger before he expressed his undeniable irritation. "Um, listen, Bob, Mike, or whatever your name is, I've had a hell of a morning, and right now I have no time for a bunch of small talk. How about giving me a few minutes to think, alright, buddy?"

"Oh, that is perfectly alright, *buddy,*" Tom replied with more than a hint of sarcasm. Then, looking Alex straight in the eye, he suddenly shifted into full professional mode and said, "Thank you for taking the time to come in today, but I don't want to waste your time or mine. Alex, it's safe to say that you're not a good fit for this position…or this company, for that matter. It's a shame, really. I had high expectations for you when we received your email last week saying you wanted to join us."

Confused, Alex shook his head. "What? Wait…oh man, you're Tom, THE Tom, I'm so sorry. I didn't know," he stammered in a futile attempt to repair the damage he'd caused.

The employer ended the interview by pointing his index finger toward the door, and in no uncertain terms, he rose to leave, but not before Alex noticed the lanyard hanging around the leader's neck. It was right there in plain view: Tom Benoit, Founder, Quark Capital. He could have kicked himself—the nametag had been right there, front and center, and if he'd only paid attention, he would've seen it.

*What on earth just happened?* he thought. *There's no way this was my fault…I didn't know.*

That's precisely what he told the receptionist on the way out.

"Why didn't you tell me that guy was the person I was meeting?"

"But I did. I directed you to meet him on the sofa and said I believed he was ready for you," she answered. "I apologize if you didn't hear me."

Alex didn't bother replying. His chin dropped to his chest in despair. There was no use arguing, and he knew it. He'd blown the one opportunity he had—the one opportunity he'd waited so long for—and why? Because he hadn't paid attention.

Nobody had ever been more disappointed in him than he was at that moment. On the ride home, the only thing he wanted to do was to crawl back in bed and hide behind closed doors for a long, long time.

◄–––––•–––––►

Fumbling for his keys as he entered his apartment building, he was quickly reminded of the earlier encounter with his now ex-girlfriend as he opened the mailbox labeled with both their names on the front.

"Hey, Alex," waved Chuck, whose apartment was directly under Alex's. "Got a minute?"

Realizing that time was about all he had left, Alex replied, "Sure, I guess. What do you need?"

"I don't need anything. I was just wondering if you've found a new place yet," said Chuck.

"A new place? What makes you think I'm looking for a new place?"

"Are you kidding me, man? We only have three more weeks to get out," Chuck bellowed. "Haven't you read the signs?"

"What signs are you talking about?"

"The big red signs that are posted on all the doors and in the elevator. You know, the ones letting us know the building has been sold and is scheduled for demolition to make room for a strip mall," Chuck replied.

"Really?" Alex asked, obviously surprised.

"Are you alright, Alex?" his neighbor asked, obviously worried.

"Uh, yeah. I suppose with the day I'm having, I shouldn't be surprised at anything today," he muttered as he walked away.

Entering his apartment, it occurred to him that it still smelled like Katie. He stood in the doorway glancing at his surroundings and realized that in one day, he'd lost everything—his girlfriend, his dream job, and his home. It all came as such a huge shock, but he also realized it shouldn't have.

The signs had been there, where anyone could have seen them. Alex realized he'd been lost in his own little world, and as a result he had lost everything that was important to him.

"Maybe it *was* my fault," he chuckled aloud at the irony, as he placed the mail on the desk…where in plain sight a bridal magazine and a real estate brochure were opened and ear-marked for him to find.

# CHAPTER TWO

B y mid-morning the next day, the brick-paved walk-
ways in Alex's neighborhood were a bustle of activity.
Alex lived in the downtown district, which attracted
shoppers, diners, joggers, and an abundance of independent
businesses. It had been named one of the top places to live,
especially for millennials who patronized the unique bou-
tiques, spas, shops, and many eateries that called the area
home. It was so popular, in fact, that Alex feared he wouldn't
be able to find another apartment in the district. They were
snatched up as soon as they hit the market.

*I hope something turns up,* he thought as he made the return
trip to his apartment after buying his usual bagel and coffee
from the corner coffee shop. *This is a nice place to visit, but I
want to live here.*

Before he put his coffee on the counter, his phone rang.
Thinking it might be Katie calling with a change of heart, he
scrambled to look at the screen. It wasn't Katie, but his initial
disappointment was short-lived when the name Joe Landry
appeared on the screen. Joe had been Alex's supervisor in
his first job straight out of college, and had become not only
a trusted friend but a mentor and ally. Although they didn't
see each other as often as Alex would have liked, they kept in
touch on a regular basis.

"Hi, Alex," Joe greeted him.

"Joe, it's great to hear from you. How're you doing?"

"Always good," came the older man's signature response.
"I'm just calling on the off chance that you might be able to
join me for lunch today. I had an appointment cancel at the

last minute and thought it would be a great opportunity to catch up."

"Today? I'd love to. Name the time and place and I'll be there!" Alex replied.

Not having much time to spare, Alex quickly showered and shaved. Grabbing his keys on his way out the door, he realized that in his excitement to hear from Joe, he'd totally forgotten about his coffee and bagel. *Funny how a simple phone call can change a day,* he thought, thankful for the diversion from his problems.

Joe had let Alex select the restaurant, and he'd chosen a bistro about five blocks from Alex's apartment, although there was no shortage of places to dine. Wherever you looked, the streets were lined with steak and seafood restaurants, cafes, pizzerias, delis, burger joints, and bakeries. There was a unique assortment of Italian, Mexican, Irish, American, and Asian cuisine, all within walking distance. Again, Alex was grateful he'd been able to live in an area so rich in so many cultures, both the usual and the unexpected. He doubted he would find a similar experience elsewhere.

The sign over the door read "The Parisian," and Alex entered to find Joe waiting inside.

"Nice choice, Alex," he gave his approval as his eyes swept across the bistro. "Really reminds me of an authentic Paris café. If you haven't been to one, I highly recommend it."

"Glad you like it, Joe," Alex replied. "Let's grab a table and catch up."

After their server took their orders, they did just that. Joe told Alex what he'd been doing for the last several months. Joe was a frequent speaker at business and community events, and in his down time, he visited his grandchildren and still kept his weekly tennis date, as he had for the past ten years. He announced that he recently had accepted an assignment to teach English as a second language and was also teaching his wife how to golf.

"Even in retirement, you don't know how to slow down, do you?" Alex laughed.

"I'm living the dream, Alex. It's what I worked for all my life. Now I get to do everything I ever wanted. So tell me, how's everything going with you? How's Katie?"

Alex could have tried to save face, but Joe knew him too well. It was better to lay it all out on the table and tell Joe everything that had transpired. He'd never been able to fool his friend before, and he knew better than to attempt it now.

For the next thirty minutes, Alex recanted the events of the day before, starting with the moment he woke up to the realization that he was losing his apartment. Looking across the table, his voice was full of resignation, "So, Joe, that's how everything's going with me. I guess you could say things are falling apart."

"The old saying is that when things are falling apart, they're actually falling into place," Joe replied.

"What do you mean?" Alex asked, confused.

"This could be the greatest opportunity of your lifetime. Alex, let me ask you, what would life be if it were completely opposite of what it is, what it has been?"

Alex paused, considering his answer. "Well, Joe, I guess I would have freedom."

"What would that look like?" Joe asked, leaning forward with obvious interest.

"I'd probably sell all of my stuff and do some traveling—you know, see authentic Parisian cafes, like you recommended. I'd see the world and everything I've been missing. Maybe I'd realize I've been grinding away for nothing," Alex admitted.

"Why don't you do that? What's stopping you?"

Before he could answer, Alex's phone rang. Seeing the caller, Alex excused himself. "Hey, I've got to take this. I'll be right back."

"Alex Best," he answered.

"Alex, this is Emily from Dr. Armstrong's office. The results came in from your tests last week. The doctor would like to see you this afternoon. Can you be here at 2:30?"

"You can't just tell me the results over the phone?"

"No. The doctor insisted on seeing you—today, if at all possible."

Agreeing to be there, Alex returned to the table and apologized to Joe for the interruption. Joe picked up their conversation right where they'd left off.

"Alex, this is your chance to do what you've always wanted. The perfect opportunity may never come again. I encourage you to consider it."

"That's good advice, Joe," remarked Alex. "You're a great friend and mentor. I know you wouldn't steer me wrong."

"From experience, I can tell you that many receive great advice, but few profit from it. Right now, *you* are your own greatest mentor. Alex, you know what you need, go take action."

Alex considered his words for a moment, then replied, "I'm going to do that, Joe."

"That's good to know," Joe said, picking up the bill. "Lunch is on me. I hate to eat and run, Alex, but Cathy and I have a tee time on the back nine, and I don't want to be late."

◄-----◆-----►

Promptly at 2:30, the nurse opened the door to the waiting room. "Alex," she announced.

Alex followed her down the hallway and into an examining room. "The doctor will be with you in just a moment," she said.

Ten minutes later, Dr. Armstrong entered the room. He sat on a chair and wasted no time.

"Alex, from time to time in my profession, I have to tell someone something I know they're not going to want to hear.

I have found it's best to just get to the bottom line. The reality is you have a rare retina disease with several other complicating conditions, which puts you in jeopardy of being rendered blind. Unfortunately, there's nothing we can do right now but monitor your vision. Whether or not the disease progresses within a year will tell us if you're going to be blind or if your sight will be spared," the doctor said.

"Wait, what? Blind? As in, I won't be able to see for the rest of my life? No, that can't be. I don't understand," Alex rambled in disbelief. Taking a deep breath, he looked up at the doctor and asked, "Are you sure there's nothing you can do?"

"I'm sure. Only time will tell if the disease will progress or not. We will just have to wait a year for the verdict," the doctor replied. "Here is a copy of your test results. Call me if you need anything," the doctor added, patting Alex's arm before exiting the room.

That night Alex sat on his balcony, looking over the shops and sights below. He thought about Joe's advice, and his mind replayed the news the doctor had shared. He reflected on the irony of not seeing the signs around him and now he might actually be losing his sight. Suddenly he realized that Joe was right. If he only had a year left to see, the events that had fallen into place gave him the perfect opportunity to travel the world and see the sights he'd always wanted to…while he could.

With that realization, his journey began.

# CHAPTER THREE

The next three weeks were a whirlwind of activity. Alex had been fortunate to be able to sell his car and most of his belongings rather quickly. Thank goodness his ex had an eye for interior design and had been the one who decorated the place, or he would have probably been stuck with the four brown Lazy Boy recliners that he had when he entered their relationship.

The rest of the time had been spent packing and cleaning, erasing any signs that he had lived in the apartment that, without furnishings, now seemed bleak and barren. Taking one last walkthrough what had been his home for the last four years, Alex was ready to leave the past behind. It was time for a new chapter in his life.

He traveled lightly, carrying as little baggage as possible. Everything about this trip would be minimal to stretch his dollars. In order to see and do everything he wanted, he had to save money in every way possible, and that included transportation. After boarding the plane, he took his seat between two passengers; while a window or aisle seat would have been nice, a middle seat was all he could afford.

As he wrapped the neck pillow under his chin, he listened to the flight attendant deliver her announcement.

"Ladies and gentlemen, my name is Jessica, and I'm your chief flight attendant. On behalf of the captain and the entire crew, welcome aboard Journey Airlines flight 333, nonstop service to the Dominican Republic."

Alex couldn't contain a small smile as he realized that this was actually happening. Suddenly, anxiety turned into excitement.

He was leaving everything and everyone he'd ever known for an entire year—twelve months that were certain to be full of unknowns. He'd chosen the Dominican Republic as his first destination for very good reason—and in just a few hours, he'd arrive.

◄━━━━━◆━━━━━►

Alex heard the D.R. was a tropical paradise; and as he took in the pristine white beaches and turquoise waters that stretched as far as the eye could see, he couldn't argue the fact. Resorts were favored by most people because they were all-inclusive, offering anything and everything a person could want. But Alex wanted to expand and explore beyond the touristy stuff to see as much as he could of what the island and its people had to offer.

His first stop was in Cabarete, where a walk along the water-front turned the sandy beaches into an explosion of color. It was like nothing he'd ever seen—at least, not in real life. Until this moment, his view had been limited to the screensaver he had set on his desktop for years.

Kite Beach was home to aspiring and professional kiteboarders, and Alex found himself mesmerized as the wind caught the kites and spread their vibrant wings across the skies. Alex enjoyed the vivid display as he watched from an outdoor café on the outskirts of the beach.

Remembering that he'd promised to send Joe pictures of his journey, he snapped a few on his phone and sent one to his friend with a text message that simply said, "Postcard worthy."

His reply was quick. "Kite Beach is spectacular. Some of those people will compete in the Master of the Ocean competition, but for natives of the island, it is simply a way of life. Enjoy yourself."

A smile formed on his (about to be) sunburned face as he realized that, although he was far from home, he was still connected by his magical mobile device. It was almost like being in two places at once.

Calling his server over, Alex handed him a ten spot and asked, "If I wanted to see the real Dominican Republic, where the people actually work and live, where would I go?"

"About twenty minutes to the north," he replied. "But you'll need a driver to get there. I can arrange one for you, if you'd like," he said.

---

The next morning, a young man in his early 20s was waiting at the door of the hotel. He explained that they were going to a remote area of the island, which was much different from the tourist hotspots.

He was taking Alex to a small but busy city, and from there they would travel farther inland where the beaches and palm trees were replaced with a jungle of thick, lush vegetation, untouched by modern machinery.

Leading into the city, the car maneuvered winding, single-lane dirt roads, which soon were lined with French cafes and native residents selling their wares. In awe, Alex watched people pass by on their motorbikes as they went about their everyday life. It was a stark difference in scenery from the day before, and one that Alex was fired up to experience.

He spent the next couple hours on foot, strolling past cafes, inns, and small stores. His driver acted as his tour guide, pointing out the fruit shops and *colmados,* where people gathered and shopped. To Alex, this was the heart of the island, and he found their way of life intriguing.

As they traveled farther inland, the area became even more remote. The business district was replaced by a jungle that served as the backdrop for a small village. As they came to the end of a narrow row of homes, Alex was surprised to see a bunch of children on a makeshift baseball diamond that had been hacked out of the jungle's edge.

"Hey, do me a favor and pull over," he asked, beginning to open the door before the vehicle had come to a complete stop.

There were several dozen ten-year-old boys on the field, but only one adult—a very elderly man was coaching them during their practices.

As Alex drew closer, he was surprised and shocked that he recognized the man. Now in his early 80s, the coach was a Hall of Fame baseball player who had won several World Series championships and was voted MVP of the Major Leagues multiple times.

Quite taken aback to discover the legendary sports idol in this backwater location, Alex was fascinated to watch him coach the young boys, not only in the fundamental rules of the game, but in life.

"Back him up! Back him up! That's why there are nine people on the field. You have to help each other out," he said, reminding them to communicate with each other: "Call it! Let your teammate know when you've got the ball," he yelled.

Then when the roles were reversed and the boys were at bat, he told them to offer their teammates support and encouragement. "Come on, now! Give him some confidence. Let him hear you!" he yelled, as the kids returned with "Good eye!" and "You've got this!"

But it was a lesson in perseverance that hit home with Alex.

During batting practice, the coach declared, "As an 80-year-old man with a bad back and fading eyesight, I can say with total confidence that I could get a hit off of the best young pitcher in the Major Leagues right now if you would allow me to change just one of the rules of baseball."

Alex was just as confused as the young players were by the coach's statement. In disbelief, he leaned forward to make sure he didn't miss a word.

The coach covered the side of his mouth and leaned down toward the youngsters and said, "Instead of three strikes, I get as many strikes as I want." The legend grinned as the kids started laughing.

"You would eventually hit one for sure with that deal!" one of the players barked out.

"That's right, as many strikes as I want." The wise man continued, "Boys, the important thing to remember is you don't strike out in life until you quit swinging. And if you keep at it, sooner or later, you can't help but get a hit."

It was a pivotal message, and one that Alex wanted to remember. Opening his backpack, he pulled out a pen to write it down, but with disappointment, realized he didn't have anything to write on. Then he spied his passport in the front compartment. Realizing it would have to do, he quickly opened it and next to the Dominican Republic stamp, he jotted down the message:

> *"You don't strike out until you quit swinging. Keep swinging and you're sure to get a hit."*

Reading it again, Alex suddenly realized that this piece of wisdom was one of the most valuable things he'd gotten from his experience on the island.

Reflecting back, he took ownership that the people in his past didn't quit on him—it was he who gave up on himself. That was what led them to exit—they no longer wanted to participate in unfulfilled potential.

"Holy smokes," he said out loud when he was hit with that aha moment, loud enough to cause all the kids to stop and turn their heads in his direction. Realizing he'd disrupted their practice, he got back into his ride and took one last look toward the older gentleman. The man turned and tipped the brim of his ball cap in his direction, acknowledging that he knew Alex had been listening the whole time.

With that, Alex quickly scribed a star next to the note he'd written in his passport to make sure he wouldn't forget the profound message…or the man who delivered it. At that moment it occurred to him that maybe, just maybe, it was fitting that the place he'd preserved it was on his passport, where he could take it with him on his travels around the world…and throughout his life.

# CHAPTER FOUR

T he eight-hour flight to Spain gave Alex plenty of time to research some of the sights he wanted to visit.

The architecture of the cities intrigued him, but so did the country's rich history.

In the end, he found that Barcelona and Madrid would provide him with the opportunity to experience both 16th-century architecture and local cultural festivals and celebrations.

After telling Joe how much he had enjoyed observing the lifestyle of the Dominicans, Joe told him to make sure he paid a visit to Plaza Mayor in Madrid.

"It's a world apart from the remote villages in the jungle, but I guarantee Madrid won't disappoint. While you're there, the Plaza Mayor is a must," his mentor said.

And Joe was right. While the D.R. had offered relaxation, Madrid was a pulsing center full of life and people. It was like nothing he'd ever seen.

Standing under the huge vaulted ceilings of the train station, it was the closest thing to experiencing all cultures, nationalities, and languages at the same time. It was a true Babylon city moment where all people come together and find a way to communicate and be as one.

Alex was pleased to find that many of Madrid's popular attractions were centrally located, making it easy for him to save money and travel on foot.

Here, he could walk to world-class art museums, all housed in buildings that were ancient architectural wonders—works of art in themselves. As he strolled along, he found he blended in with the crowd, which never seemed to wane. Tourists and residents intertwined in the busy streets, enjoying shopping, live entertainment, and the summer sunshine as they ate at one of the many outdoor cafes.

After perusing the typical must-see spots for a few hours, Alex stopped to order a *café con leche* at one of the sidewalk cafes. Sitting at a table, he was watching each passerby when he was approached by a young Spanish man.

"Buenos dias. May I join you?"

"Sure, I guess—I mean, of course," Alex answered, a bit taken aback since he hadn't expected company at that moment, yet he was happy to welcome the friendly face.

"Let me guess—you're a tourist," the young man stated.

"What gave me away?"

"It's a gift. Thousands of people pass through here every day, and I can identify tourists and residents very quickly. It's become a game of sorts for me. Plus, the fanny pack with the open map on the table with a camera around your neck is a dead giveaway."

They both laughed.

Alex smiled and extended his hand. "By the way, my name is Alex," he offered.

"And I'm Mateo. Welcome to Madrid, my friend."

As the two men talked, Alex told Mateo about the journey he had planned for the year. Once in a while, Mateo would interject, sharing a story or suggesting his next place to travel.

"Ultimately, you can go anywhere around the world, Alex, but to me, you've chosen wisely. Spain has it all! It's a vibrant community that is alive at all hours—day and night. Here, in the plaza of Puerta del Sol, you are in what we call the heart of our city. But there is so much more to see! If you haven't yet, don't leave without visiting the Plaza Mayor," he enthusiastically suggested.

"Yes, someone back home told me I had to go there," Alex added.

"It's the pulse of the city, man! If Puerta del Sol is the heart, Plaza Mayor is the heartbeat. The famous San Miguel Market is there, and I love it because it holds the footprint of our history. Many historic events have occurred in Plaza Mayor, including the proclamation of a new king. Oh, and the celebrations are unlike any you'll find anywhere on your travels," Mateo said.

"What kind of celebrations?" Alex asked.

"My favorite is our annual Christmas market. It's spectacular," Mateo answered. "Plaza Mayor has boasted many historic celebrations, including the canonization of saints and some of the best bullfights in Spain's history."

"Bullfights? Now that would be cool," Alex replied.

"Si. Mi *bisabuelo*, or great grandfather as you would say, was a bullfighter. But today, people prefer running with the bulls, rather than fighting them."

"Oh, yes, the running of the bulls! That's held near here, isn't it, Mateo?"

"Yes, it's held in Pamplona during the annual San Fermin Festival. It's a tradition that attracts millions from all around the world. I've never run with the bulls, though. But I will tell you that if you're going to do it, you need to make sure you learn everything about it first. I guarantee if you don't know what you're doing, the bulls are going to run you down," he said. "It's been said that this is the only sporting activity on earth where someone participating is guaranteed to end up in an ambulance."

His talk with Mateo gave Alex plenty to do during the rest of his stay in Madrid, and his new friend was correct—the Plaza was spectacular.

The square went through the middle of the city and a tree-lined street cut through the center, marking the plaza and its many shops and cafes. Visually, it was something of a postcard.

It was evident that the Plaza was designed for people to congregate and mingle, as evidenced by the stone-paved street, designed only for pedestrians. Mateo had told him that anything could be found here, from souvenirs to produce and cafes and restaurants, to fresh markets, all surrounded by marvels of construction and architecture that were the setting for some of the greatest moments in history.

It took nearly a full day to explore every corner and nook in the square, but when he was done, Alex was content that he had experienced the best that Madrid had to offer.

---

A thrill of excitement rushed over Alex the next morning as he prepared to set out for Barcelona.

Before he left, he quickly texted his friend, Joe.

"Hey, Joe. Wanted you to know I'm having a great time. Loved Madrid, now I've got to run—run with the bulls, that is!"

Alex's research showed him that Pamplona was a smaller city outside of Barcelona, where he was staying. The festival drew huge numbers of people, and many traveled by train or car during the seven-day event.

He also learned that thousands of people ran with the bulls every year, and he figured if they could do it, so could he. After all, this was a once-in-a-lifetime journey and he wanted to get everything out of it he could. But taking Mateo's advice, he first did some digging until he found someone who could offer him some tips.

"Talk to Francisco. He literally wrote the book on running with the bulls. If anyone can help you, he can," he was told.

The next question was how in the world was he going to gain access to this famous author?

On the bullet train ride toward his next location, Alex began plotting his mission to find this guy and get the inside scoop. He figured Francisco spoke to hundreds, if not thousands, about the Pamplona run, so there had to be some information about him on the Internet.

With decent WIFI on the train, he typed his name into the search bar and within a second, the famed author's website and phone number appeared.

Alex literally laughed out loud when he realized just how easy it was to locate him. *It was crazy,* he thought, realizing he'd spent hours thinking about how hard it was going to be and scheming ways to get someone to share the writer's information, when in fact, it only took the simple action of typing in his name.

*I guess it's true what they say,* Alex thought aloud. *We spend 95 percent of our time dreading something that is only 5 percent real.*

The moment Francisco answered the call, information rolled off his new friend's tongue as if scripted and memorized. He gave Alex a brief history of the run and walked him through it from beginning to end.

"You seem very knowledgeable, sir," Alex commented. "I take it you've run with the bulls yourself?"

"For more than twenty years, and I'm still standing," he chuckled.

Realizing that there is power in receiving counsel from someone who had already mastered a topic, versus someone merely giving an opinion, Alex immediately knew Francisco was the go-to source on this topic.

"Look, let me be straight with you—if I'm going to run with the bulls and have the best time, where should I stand so I can enjoy myself and not get killed?"

Francisco laughed at Alex's bluntness—spoken like a true American, he sure got right to the point. He told him exactly which area to stand in and the corners to avoid.

"Here's what you do—go to this exact location and stand in the middle. In doing so, Alex, you'll have the greatest experience, because on one side, the bulls will be running right next to you, and on the other side, people will be trampling each other. Here, you will be out of harm's way and can experience the best of both worlds. More importantly, understand this: You don't run *with* the bulls. You run *from* the bulls."

The two laughed at the distinction, before Alex said, "I've heard there will be a million people there or watching live on TV. How many people are actually participating, though?"

"While, yes, you are correct in that over one million people are spectators; watching other people do it. But at most, only around 3,000 people participate in any given run. That's just the way life is."

Alex took a mental note of Francisco's words while he thanked him for his generosity. As soon as he arrived at his hotel, he opened his passport, and next to his newest stamp, he wrote:

*"Life isn't a spectator sport. Get out and DO it!
Very few people participate, while most are watching from the sidelines."*

◄––––––◆––––––►

Alex spent the rest of the week sightseeing and making sure he was prepared for the run. The San Fermin Festival opened on July 7, and he gathered with the crowd, hoping to watch the first running so he knew what to expect.

He kept his eyes on the people standing right where Francisco told him to go and their outcome. Francisco was right. If he did exactly as he'd suggested, Alex was confident he could successfully run "from" the bulls and make it out alive—while experiencing the rush of a lifetime.

The next morning, adrenalin was flowing as Alex took his place among the throngs of people waiting for the bulls to be released.

It all happened so quickly—the rockets were fired and the people started running; the sound from the crowd was tremendous as 3,000 people charged through the streets with 1,000-pound beasts on their heels.

Staying on course, Alex kept an even pace and his eyes on his goal. Excitement and adrenaline drove him the whole way to the bullfighting stadium, which signified the end of the run.

It was the longest four minutes of his life, but the most exhilarating and rewarding four minutes he'd ever experienced. That's when Alex realized that he was capable of doing anything, but he had to "participate" in order to reap the rewards.

# CHAPTER FIVE

Alex's latest adventure had been packed with activity, some of which he participated in and some that he observed. Spain had given him some great memories and a personal milestone. Running with—or from—the bulls was something he'd never forget.

The power of seeking expert counsel was a lesson learned that he would revisit for the rest of his life.

As one could imagine, the bus ride to the Netherlands was long, but Alex simply couldn't justify the cost of a plane ticket. Besides, it gave him an opportunity to sit back and reflect on his travels and get some much needed rest. His adrenaline had been riding high; it was time to let it come down.

Closing his eyes, Alex leaned back in his seat, and his imagination conjured up a vision of Holland. Not knowing what to expect, glimpses of brightly colored tulip fields and storybook windmills flashed through his mind. It was a quiet and pleasant vision that calmed him to the point that it lulled him to sleep.

When he stepped off the bus some fifteen hours later, Alex stood in the middle of Amsterdam. His legs were a bit wobbly from sitting still for such an extended period of time; trying to stand upright made him feel like he was in the center of a scene from the movie *Bambi*.

*I must be the only person on foot,* he thought. *Everyone I see is riding a bicycle.* There were more bikes than cars on the street; and as he looked up and down the block, there were bike stands outside every shop and restaurant.

Then it occurred to him that pedal power would be a great way to get around and do some sightseeing; and as he suspected, he didn't have to look very far to find one to rent.

"Take whichever one you want from the rack out front," the clerk said, handing him back his ID and credit card. "Oh, and here's your lock and key. You have to return those, as well, in order to get your deposit back."

Alex rode around the city streets for an hour before stopping to get a bite to eat at a small Dutch café. The menu offered a variety of items, but to his surprise, nearly all of them consisted of breads and cheeses. *Just pretend you're eating a cheeseburger, without the burger,* he laughed to himself as he ordered his lunch.

After eating, he decided to veer out of the business district, hoping he didn't have to travel very far to see some of the countryside. At the edge of town, a tour bus sat next to the curb that advertised tours every two hours for five euro a person. Locking his bike in the closest stand, Alex pulled out his cash and boarded the bus, ready for his next adventure.

The tour guide was a friendly and knowledgeable woman who pointed out landmarks on their scenic route.

"To your right, you'll find the Herengracht, also known as the Gentleman's Canal, which was dug in the 17<sup>th</sup> century. The mansions which line it were homes to the elite and prestigious—mayors, government officials, and wealthy merchants. To this day, a home on this canal is one of the most desirable places to live," the guide said. "As we round the curve, we move away from the canal, and you'll soon view hundreds of acres of tulip fields. From March to May, more than seven billion tulips bloom here, attracting tourists from around the world."

As Alex gazed out the window, he admired the country and its rich history.

It was a world of difference from Barcelona. Gone was the bustle of activity, replaced by a slower pace and a gentler lifestyle.

"Why did people wear wooden shoes?" asked one of the other seven passengers aboard the bus.

"Ah, that's a good question. The Dutch *used* to wear wooden shoes. Some called them clogs, and others called the sabots. Amsterdam is below sea level, and there is a lot of water. Both fishermen and farmers wore shoes made of wood to protect their feet. Wood was less penetrable than leather, and because it is porous, it absorbed perspiration, allowing the foot to breathe. Here's a bit of trivia—legend has it that a group of disgruntled factory employees once threw their sabots into machinery in an effort to deliberately disrupt production. To this day, that is how many believe the word 'sabotage' came about. However, its origin is far less dramatic and destructive and simply means an intentional reduction in productivity during a time when, yes, workers wore wooden shoes," she explained.

Alex listened intently as their guide shared Amsterdam's history and folklore as the tour bus drove past homes and farms, where the countryside was dotted with, yes, windmills old and new. It was an enjoyable afternoon and one he regretted coming to an end when the bus returned to its station.

Alex took the key out of the zipped compartment and sat his backpack against a building while he fidgeted with his bike lock, which didn't turn right away. People came and went around him, parking and picking up their bikes, as he tried without success to open the lock for what seemed like an eternity. Finally, he put the key back in, figuring he'd give it one more try before asking for help, and the lock turned with so much ease that Alex was sure there had to be some trick to it.

Not wanting to repeat that scenario, he decided it was time to return the bike. Reaching down, he grabbed his backpack and rode back into town.

◆–––––◆–––––◆

"Here you go," the clerk said as she returned his deposit for the rental.

"Thanks," he said. "Maybe you can help me. I'm looking for a good place to eat this evening and a hotel or hostel where I can stay. Can you recommend an inexpensive spot in the area?"

As she gave Alex the name of an inn, he opened his backpack to put his money in his wallet. But his wallet wasn't in the backpack. In fact, it wasn't even his backpack!

Oh, it looked the same—it was black, but it certainly wasn't his. His heart sank a beat as he pulled out the contents—a bright pink and white striped bikini, sunscreen, sunglasses, flip flops, and a book that had been earmarked and highlighted to the extreme.

*Oh no. What am I going to do? I grabbed the wrong one. Everything I have is in it—my clothes, my money, phone, passport, my identification. Darn it!*

Devastated, Alex started walking back to the bus stop, the last place he'd seen his backpack. He couldn't believe he'd been so careless. This time, he had nobody else to blame—he did this to himself!

*Why can't I learn to pay attention? I should know better by now. But no, it wasn't enough that I was blind to all the signs that Katie gave me or the fact that I botched up the best job opportunity and destroyed any chance of getting my dream job. Oh, no, now I've really gone and done it. I'm halfway around the world and don't know a single soul. I have no money and no ID. I don't have a passport and can't go anywhere. Hell, I can't even call anyone for help. It's ironic that the tour guide talked about sabotage today because here I am...sabotaging my own life.*

Alex beat himself up until he got to the bus stop and realized that the wall was empty. There were no backpacks leaning against it, none whatsoever. There he was, holding pink bikini girl's backpack while she was somewhere holding everything he had to his name. And he had no idea who she was or how to find her.

In full panic mode, Alex went through her backpack once again, hoping to find something, anything with a name on it. The book!

Quickly, he flipped through the pages to see if her name was scribbled in it, but he had no such luck.

*Great, what am I going to do?* he asked himself as he sat down on the curb. *I could call Joe, but I don't have a phone. No, stupid me left it in the front zipper of my backpack.*

Suddenly he realized in his state of panic he hadn't opened the small front compartment in the backpack he was holding. Maybe, just maybe, pink bikini girl kept her phone there too, and maybe just maybe...

The sleek rose gold iPhone he pulled out was the best thing he'd ever seen—like holding the key to the meaning of life.

He held his breath when he pushed the home button, hoping that there was a remote chance that the phone wasn't locked. He only had to make one phone call—just one. He had to call his phone and just hope and pray that bikini girl answered it.

To his surprise, the phone wasn't locked. Fingers shaking, he punched in his number and waited for an answer.

"Hello?" answered a frantic female voice.

"Thank God you answered. Don't hang up—my name is Alex, and I think you have my backpack," he said.

"I sure do. I have your wallet and your passport, and all kinds of stuff. What happened? Why did you take my backpack?" she asked, irritation now in her voice.

"I didn't *take* your backpack. It was a mix up. They're both black, and I just grabbed the wrong one. I guess I wasn't paying attention," he replied.

"You sure weren't. So what are we going to do—where are you? How can I get my stuff…and my phone. I need my phone," she said. "Can you bring it to me?"

"That's the thing—I can't. You see, I'm a tourist. I don't have a car or even a bike. I don't even have a place to stay. You have my wallet and all of my money…and without it, I don't have any way to bring you anything. I'm stuck here at the bike rack next to the bus stop," Alex explained.

"Okay. Do me a favor and stay there. No, wait, I have an errand to run first, but I can meet you at the café just down the street at 6 o'clock. Does that work?" she asked.

"Okay. I'll be there," he agreed. "Hey, before you hang up, I need to know your name."

"Jade—my name is Jade," she said. "I'll see you at 6—please be there."

According to the time on Jade's phone, Alex had more than an hour to kill before exchanging their bags. He looked around and found a bench to sit on, figuring he could pass some time watching passersby. After a few minutes, though, boredom set in and he decided to go to the café early. He was thirsty and with the money he'd gotten back when he returned the bike, he could get something cold to drink.

Sitting at a table near the door where he could be seen right away, he looked for something to do. He could use Jade's phone to get on the Internet, but that felt like an invasion of her privacy. But then again so was rummaging through her belongings, pink bikini, sunscreen, and all. But there was a book, maybe he could kill some time leafing through it.

He reached into the backpack and pulled out the book. For the first time he noticed the title, *How to Find the Ideal Date.*

*Interesting,* he thought as he flipped through the pages, flipping to the ones with corners turned down and others that were highlighted.

As his eyes passed over the content, he realized what he was reading. It was a book that revealed how women thought and what they truly wanted; and as he read, he realized that he had been doing just the opposite.

*That explains a lot,* he laughed to himself.

Everything he'd done in the past had been contrary to what women were looking for in a relationship. On one particular earmarked page, the author advised that men should do what women had been doing for years—instead of talking about themselves, they should flip the conversation and let the woman share her views fully.

Page after page, it was a true eye-opener.

The café door opened, and Alex quickly shoved the book back in the backpack as a young blonde woman carrying one that looked like his walked in.

Seeing hers on the table, she walked directly to him.

"You must be Alex. I'm Jade, and this," she said, "this…is your backpack."

"Thank you. And here's yours. Please accept my apology for making you go to all this trouble. There really is no excuse…"

"It's okay. Accidents happen. I'm sorry that I wasn't very friendly when you called," she said. "I was literally freaking out. You don't know how lost I felt before you called."

"I think I do," Alex admitted. "And I totally understand. I was pretty angry with myself, too," he laughed. "Can I get you something to drink?"

"Well, I guess, if you don't mind," Jade replied as she sat across from him. "So, Alex, tell me about yourself. Your ID says you're from the States. Are you on vacation? Studying abroad?"

"Neither, actually. I guess you could say I'm on a hiatus of sorts," he answered. "Back home, I was about to start a new job search until I realized…"

Then it hit him. He was doing it again, not expressing interest in anyone but himself. Remembering that the book said to flip the conversation, he took the lead.

"Enough about me. Tell me about yourself, Jade. What do you do, besides sunbathe?" he smiled.

Their laughter broke the ice, and Alex found himself genuinely interested in the blonde, blue-eyed woman across from him. He learned that she owns a business that makes skincare products, and the sunscreen in her backpack was part of her line.

"I'm impressed. You're pretty young to have your own company," he said.

"Well, I'm a co-owner. When I completed college, a girl-friend and I developed the line and opened a shop in an old, neglected building. It didn't matter what it looked like, since all of our sales were online. But the building was so dilapidated and run-down that it caught on fire a couple years ago and nearly put us out of business."

"That must have been terrible."

"That's what I thought, too, at first anyway. But it forced us to decide if our business was just a hobby or if we were serious about it," Jade replied.

"So what did you do?"

"We built a bigger, better facility. It's not huge by any means, but it allowed us to increase our production and our product line. In the end, I guess what seemed devastating turned out to be a blessing in disguise," she said. "Now we employ people from the town, and we are growing a little bit each month."

As Alex listened, he realized that maybe being careless was a blessing in disguise. Otherwise, he wouldn't have found himself sitting across from this smart, interesting woman—who by the way, just so happened to have the cutest spattering of freckles across the top of her cheeks.

"Hey, Jade, I know you don't really know me, but can I take you out to dinner? I've put you to a lot of trouble, and it's the least I can do. Besides, I'm starving—all I've had to eat today is bread and cheese," he said.

"So you've become a connoisseur of the Dutch breakfast and lunch?" she laughed. "I'd be happy to join you. There's a great restaurant around the corner. Let's go."

As they rose to leave, Alex grabbed his backpack and flung it over his shoulder, before suddenly remembering...he gently sat the backpack down on the table, unzipped it and peeked inside to make sure this time he didn't make the same mistake twice.

# CHAPTER
# SIX

The night before was magical. It was a fate-filled alliance that would surely be a highlight when looking back on this adventure. Alex's time with his new friend, Jade, was something that dreams are made of.

After their dinner, they found themselves walking the streets for hours and in doing so, realized all that they had in common. It occurred to Alex how funny it was that he found himself halfway around the world, only to meet someone who understands him in a way that's hard to comprehend.

Excited to reconnect once more, they agreed to meet up again the next day, after his preplanned field trip out of the local area.

———◆◆◆———

The recommended hotel served its purpose. Although it had been referred to as a "suite," his room was small, with more of a hostel feel than a three-star hotel, with barely enough room to house a bed and dresser. It wasn't the Hilton, but the price was right, and Alex knew that he had to be frugal whenever he could.

"Will you be staying another night, sir?" the desk clerk asked when he went down to the lobby for his complimentary croissant and cup of morning joe.

"I think I will," Alex replied, remembering that he had agreed to meet Jade for dinner again that evening. "I do need help, though. Can you tell me where to find the train station?"

"Where are you going?" the clerk asked.

"Tillburg," he answered. "Actually, I'll be visiting the Meta Maze at Doloris. Have you heard of it?"

"Oh, yes. It's quite an experience and not difficult to find at all. The central train station will take you right there. Let me see," he said as he thumbed through some papers. "Ah, yes, here is the train schedule. The station is within walking distance, just a few blocks to the north. You can't miss it."

Thanking him, Alex sat down with a cup of coffee and searched the Internet for the Meta Maze, which Jade had recommended he visit while he was in the Netherlands.

"Is it really a maze?" Alex shouted to the man behind the counter.

"Yes, some people refer to it as a labyrinth," echoing the same unnecessarily loud tone, considering they were no more than ten feet apart. "Regardless, it's an experience you'll never forget. It's perfect if you're on your own because they don't allow people to enter together. Oh, and let me forewarn you, no phones, watches, or cameras are allowed in the maze."

"I guess that's a good thing," Alex laughed. "If I don't have them with me, maybe I won't manage to lose them. Tell me more."

"The Meta Maze is something you have to see with your very own eyes. I'll just leave it at that," he replied.

The clerk was right.

The train took him directly to Tillburg and stopped an hour later right outside Doloris, the event center that was home to the Meta Maze. After purchasing his ticket, Alex was pulled aside and to his surprise, a blindfold was placed over his eyes.

Alex couldn't help but ponder the possibility of losing his sight permanently as he experienced the world around him wearing a blindfold.

"Don't worry," the woman said. "This is temporary. It will be removed after you've entered the Maze."

He listened intently as he received his instructions. There were 40 rooms, and to navigate his journey through them, he had to pay attention to detail. It would entail crawling and climbing, and while it wasn't frightening, he should expect the unexpected.

In the back of his mind, he expected nothing more than the mazes he'd entered in amusement parks and cornfields as a child, but nothing could have prepared him for the maze he entered. Once his blindfold was removed, he immediately felt like he'd entered the bowels of a sculpture, surrounded by sights and sounds that consumed his senses.

*It's like a wonderland,* he thought. *Like Alice going down the rabbit hole.*

His journey took him into what he could only describe as another dimension, and he became totally immersed in the art and amazing visuals at every turn. With no sense of time or place, he maneuvered tight hallways and found himself literally walking through walls and slipping through loopholes. From time to time, mysterious objects interjected him on his path.

To say he was taken out of his comfort zone was an understatement. Yes, he was apprehensive and his senses were heightened more than he'd ever known them to be. But he wasn't scared, just on high alert and mesmerized by the art, the intensity, and the mystery that fully encapsulated and surrounded him.

In a different realm, Alex found himself seeing and sensing everything through an entirely foreign perspective. It was surreal, but in ways that went beyond what his eyes could see. There was a deep awareness of all his senses, one that made him consider the possibility that losing his eyesight could actually be a blessing, something he had never before contemplated.

If exploring and experiencing the unexpected had been the reason he traveled around the world, his mission was accomplished.

Having lost all sense of space, time, and reality, Alex finally emerged into daylight and the real world. But his experience was far from over, as he entered the largest rooftop restaurant he'd ever seen. Here he could literally enjoy food and drinks from anywhere around the world, all in one place.

◄--------◆--------►

"Did you enjoy the maze?" asked a man standing nearby.

"Oh yeah, it was amazing. I didn't know what to expect around each corner. It was like when the music stops, you wondered what was going to happen next!"

"I agree. We've been here several times, and each time we discover something new," he said. "We Americans get the biggest kick out of this place. I can see you are from the States as well! Would you like to join me and my wife for a quick bite and share some travel stories?"

"If I wouldn't be intruding, I'd love to," Alex readily agreed, welcoming the company, as he felt a need to talk about what he'd just experienced.

For the next hour, they ate and compared their observations and emotions while they enjoyed the flavors of virtually any cuisine they could ask for.

"I just can't get over how each of us interpreted all the facets of the maze differently," Alex pointed out.

"That isn't surprising at all. You see, everything is subject to interpretation, and our interpretation is based on our experiences. While we may see things at the same time, it's unlikely that we will see them through the same lens at the same time," the gentleman said with a southern drawl, leaving Alex to figure they were from Texas or thereabouts.

"I know what you mean. It's hard to explain, but I don't think I've ever seen anything like it. Perhaps, I never will again," Alex said, almost thinking out loud.

It was early evening when he returned to the inn and contacted Jade, as he had promised to do.

"I'm sorry. I thought I'd be back earlier. It seems that I lost all sense of time," he said.

"Not at all. That's what the maze is intended to do, Alex. Time becomes fluid once you enter it—thus the no-watch rule."

Having had a full day, Alex opted for a quiet evening and suggested a walk through one of the nearby gardens, where they could leisurely talk. Arriving a few minutes early, he sat on a bench and pulled out his passport to document his latest travels.

Wanting to remember the man's words that afternoon, he pulled out his pen and wrote:

> *Doloris Meta Maze, Tillburg, Netherlands: We may all see the same things at the same time, but we won't see them through the same set of lenses.*

Reflecting on how profound those words were, he turned his attention to the day before and his adventures from the time he arrived in Amsterdam, including his oversight in taking the wrong backpack. Thankfully, that had ended well—even better than he could have expected, given the fact that he wouldn't have met Jade otherwise.

"What are you doing, Alex?" she asked as she approached the bench.

"This? It's nothing really. Just jotting a few things down in my passport," he answered.

"In your passport? Mind if I take a look?" she asked.

Alex walked her through the thoughts he'd preserved next to the stamps depicting his travels. Listening intently, she didn't say a word until he was finished.

"That's awesome, Alex. What a cool way to document your travels. So, tell me, have you written anything about me in there?" she teased.

"Not yet. As a matter of fact, I was about to, but I couldn't figure out just what I wanted to say. My first thought was that I had learned a lesson about sabotaging my life, but it didn't seem to capture everything," he shared.

"Well, losing your backpack wasn't all bad. After all, you met me because of it," she smiled.

"I was thinking the same thing. So maybe it was all good— an all-clouds-have-a-silver-lining kind of thing," he said.

"Hmmm, maybe. It reminds me of something my grand-mother used to say, 'If you want to find your fortune, look first at your misfortune.'"

Taken aback at her words, Alex turned to Jade and said, "Your grandmother sounds like a very wise woman."

"She was, indeed. She always believed that everything hap-pens for a reason, and it's the lessons that life taught us that were the most valuable ones we'd ever receive," she said.

They spent the next couple hours walking and talking. Still wowed by his experience at the maze, he enthusiastically answered Jade's questions, but then remembered it wasn't all about him. Turning the tables, he listened while she described her first visit to the maze.

"I don't know how to describe it, Alex. It was almost like seeing things for the very first time," she said softly. "And when you're done, you want to relive it in your mind."

"Or one could say it's like seeing things for the last time," Alex interjected. "And falling short of being able to aptly preserve it."

He wasn't sure if the day had left his senses in overload or if he just felt comfortable talking to Jade, but either way, he opened up and told her about his potential eye disease.

"That's why I'm here. I'm taking the opportunity to see the world now, just in case…," he said.

"Oh no! Alex, is that why you grabbed my backpack by mistake, because you couldn't see clearly? And I blamed you…" her words were wrought with guilt.

"No! My vision is fine—for now. It was an oversight, something I'm obviously quite good at," he laughed. "I guess I felt like I should be honest with you. I didn't mean to worry you or make you feel bad."

Letting out a relieved sigh, Jade suddenly blurted, "I have an idea! Alex, if you want to see the world, I want to show it to you! I've been across Europe and would be an excellent tour guide. Let's go all in and see it all! It'll be fun! And I know just where to start. I want to take you to the greatest show on earth!"

"On Broadway?" he laughed.

"No, silly. Germany. Alex, we're going to see the biggest, grandest circus you'll ever see!"

◆－－－－－◆－－－－－▶

That night Alex pulled out his passport once again and penned the words that came to him—words that had eluded him just hours before:

> *"If you want to find your fortune, look no further than your misfortune."*
>
> —Jade, Amsterdam